U.S. HISTORY
TIMELINES

American Revolution
1754-1784

Helen Lepp Friesen

MEDIA ENHANCED BOOKS
AV2 BY WEIGL
ADDED VALUE • AUDIO VISUAL

www.av2books.com

AV² provides enriched content that supplements and complements this book Weigl's AV² books strive to create inspired learning and engage young minds in a total learning experience.

Your AV² Media Enhanced books come alive with...

 Audio
Listen to sections of the book read aloud.

 Key Words
Study vocabulary, and complete a matching word activity.

 Video
Watch informative video clips.

 Quizzes
Test your knowledge.

Embedded Weblinks
Gain additional information for research.

 Slide Show
View images and captions, and prepare a presentation.

Try This!
Complete activities and hands-on experiments.

... and much, much more!

Go to **www.av2books.com**, and enter this book's unique code.

BOOK CODE

R 8 3 6 3 8 6

AV² by Weigl brings you media enhanced books that support active learning.

Published by AV² by Weigl
350 5th Avenue, 59th Floor
New York, NY 10118
Websites: www.av2books.com   www.weigl.com

Library of Congress Control Number: 2014933473

ISBN 978–1–48960–712–6 (hardcover)
ISBN 978–1–48960–713–3 (softcover)
ISBN 978–1–48960–714–0 (single–user eBook)
ISBN 978–1–48960–715–7 (multi–user eBook)

Printed in the United States of America in North Mankato, Minnesota
1 2 3 4 5 6 7 8 9 0   18 17 16 15 14

052014
WEP301113

Project Coordinator: Aaron Carr
Editors: Pamela Dell and Frances Purslow
Designer: Mandy Christiansen

Every reasonable effort has been made to trace ownership and to obtain permission to reprint copyright material. The publishers would be pleased to have any errors or omissions brought to their attention so that they may be corrected in subsequent printings.

Weigl acknowledges Getty Images as the primary image supplier for this title.

CONTENTS

Road to Revolution

The American **Revolution** began in 1775. At that time, Great Britain's King George III ruled the Thirteen **Colonies** on the Atlantic coast of North America. The colonists wanted to break away from British rule. They wanted the right to govern themselves.

However, the events that led to the American Revolution began many years before. The settlers who lived in North America in the 1700s had come from several countries in Europe. Many had left Europe seeking greater freedom than they had at home. The first British settlements were in modern-day Virginia and Massachusetts. The French settled first in the cities of Quebec and Montreal in Canada. Before long, Great Britain and France were fighting over territory. Many American Indians joined the side of the French. In 1754, the British and French fought each other in the French and Indian War.

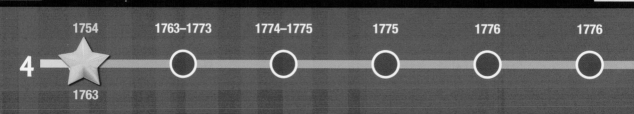

EUROPEAN SETTLERS BEGAN coming to North America in the early 1500s. They came mostly from Great Britain, France, Spain, Sweden, and Holland.

General Louis-Joseph, Marquis de Montcalm, commanded French troops defending Quebec City.

FRENCH AND INDIAN WAR

In the early 1750s, an intense struggle broke out between France and Great Britain. Each side wanted Ohio River Valley land near today's Pittsburgh, Pennsylvania. This struggle led to the British formally declaring war in 1756.

The war lasted seven years. It was a long and costly fight for control of North America. Often referred to as the Seven Years' War, it was called the French and Indian War in the colonies.

On September 17, 1759, British forces had a major breakthrough. They took Québec City from the French after a successful battle on the nearby Plains of Abraham. However, both the French and British commanders were killed in the battle.

On September 8, 1760, the British seized Montreal. The city had been France's last major claim in North America. The war officially ended in 1763 when the **Treaty** of Paris was signed. Great Britain had achieved a major victory.

Critical Events

The French and Indian War ended with Great Britain gaining control of North American land that used to belong to France. A huge amount of American territory was ruled by British **parliament**. In 1763, King George III issued a royal **proclamation**. This document outlined where settlers could live. It banned settlement west of the Appalachian Mountains. This was to be American Indian land. Colonists already living there had to move. The king hoped this would ease tensions between American Indians and settlers.

As well, British parliament passed many harsh laws. This included new taxes to help pay the cost of the French and Indian War. The money collected in taxes also paid for the army needed to defend and protect the colonies.

1754–1763   DECEMBER 13, 1763   1774–1775   1775   1776   1776

DECEMBER 16, 1773

The British parliament passed the following laws. These laws were not popular in the colonies. Some of the new laws lasted only a couple of years before being cancelled.

SUGAR ACT OF 1764

The Sugar Act added extra charges to products such as sugar, **textiles**, coffee, wine, and dye. The British used the act to force colonies to trade with Great Britain and her colonies instead of with other countries.

CURRENCY ACT OF 1764

In 1764, there were no gold or silver mines in North America. These metals were not available for making coins. So, the colonies printed paper money called bills of credit. With the Currency Act, Great Britain controlled how much paper money the colonies could print and what it could be used for.

STAMP ACT OF 1765

The Stamp Act required that many printed materials in the colonies be produced on stamped paper from London. The money raised by this new law paid for the 10,000 soldiers stationed in the colonies. The colonists did not feel that the army was needed. This act only lasted one year.

BOSTON TEA PARTY, 1773

Great Britain also placed a tax on tea. This angered the colonists. In protest, several New England colonists formed a group called the Sons of Liberty.

On the night of December 16, 1773, the Sons of Liberty dressed as Mohawk Indians. They climbed aboard three British ships anchored in Boston Harbor. Once onboard, they dumped the ships' cargo—342 crates of tea—into the harbor.

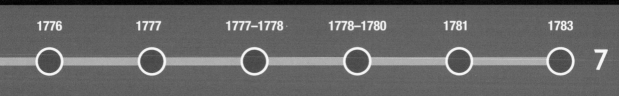

Revolution Begins

The American colonies were far from Great Britain. By 1774, many of the colonists did not want to be ruled by a king. These **Patriots** began planning their road to freedom.

On the evening of April 18, 1775, hundreds of British troops left Boston, Massachusetts. The soldiers planned to destroy the Patriots' **arsenal** at Concord. They also hoped to capture Patriot leaders Samuel Adams and John Hancock in nearby Lexington.

These actions brought the British–American conflict to a head. The next morning, April 19, was historic. About 70 armed colonists faced British troops on Lexington Green. Soon, the first shots rang out. The American Revolution had begun.

NO ONE KNOWS for sure who fired first at Lexington Green, but that gunfire made history. It became known as "the shot heard 'round the world."

| 1754–1763 | 1763–1773 | 1774 | 1775 | 1776 | 1776 |

APRIL 18, 1775

An Historic Ride

On the night of April 18, 1775, three men helped alert the Patriots in Lexington and Concord. They were William Dawes, Samuel Prescott, and Paul Revere. Revere is the best known of the three.

Before leaving Boston, Revere arranged a signal to let the Patriots know the route British troops were taking. If the British were coming by land, one lit lantern would be hung in Boston's Old North Church bell tower. If they were coming by boat across the Charles River, here would be two lanterns.

That night, two lanterns shone in the bell tower. The troops were coming by water. Revere arrived in Lexington in time to alert Adams and Hancock. The two men fled. Shortly afterward, Revere was arrested. The British soon let him go. They were more concerned about getting ready for battle. Prescott and Dawes escaped into the night.

George Washington, Commander in Chief

During the 1750s, George Washington was a loyal British citizen. He had fought for Great Britain in the French and Indian War. Afterward, he hoped to become an officer in the British army. He was turned down. Angered, Washington began to change his **loyalties**.

After the Lexington battle, one thing was clear to the Patriots. They needed their own army. In May 1775, the **Second Continental Congress** chose Washington as commander in chief of the Continental Army.

For the next six years, Washington led the Patriots in many battles against Great Britain. He was a bold leader. The troops were not well-trained or well-equipped, yet they had some early victories.

AS THE FIRST president of the United States, Washington is sometimes called the "Father of the Country."

THE BATTLE OF Bunker Hill was the bloodiest of the entire American Revolution.

Bunker Hill

On the evening of June 16, 1775, Patriot troops were ordered to Bunker Hill near Boston. There, they could watch for British movement in the surrounding area below. For some unclear reason, the Patriots marched past Bunker Hill. They took over Breed's Hill instead.

The next morning, the Patriots faced the British in battle. They fled after just three hours. The British won and took control of Breed's Hill. The conflict became incorrectly known as the Battle of Bunker Hill.

Despite their retreat, the Patriots gained confidence from the battle. They saw that they could stand up to the British army.

BATTLE LOSSES

PATRIOTS – More than 400 deaths and injuries

BRITISH – 1,054 deaths and injuries

The Push for Freedom

As time passed, the Patriots became more certain. The American colonies must be free. In the late spring of 1776, one of these Patriots had a bold idea. His name was Richard Henry Lee.

Lee, from Virginia, was a member of the Continental Congress. In Congress on June 7, Lee presented a formal **proposal**. It was known as the Lee Resolution. It suggested that the "United Colonies" **declare** their **independence** from Great Britain. Most of the **delegates** to Congress were in favor of the proposal. A few still wanted to make peace with Great Britain.

ON JULY 2, 1776, the delegates for 12 of the 13 colonies voted in favor of Lee's proposal for independence. The delegates from New York did not vote.

1754–1763   1763–1773   1774–1775   1775   **JUNE 7, 1776**   1776

JULY 2, 1776

Thomas Paine was a Patriot and a writer. One of his bestselling pamphlets was titled *The American Crisis*. Paine strongly supported independence for the United States. In his writings, he **criticized** King George III and the **loyalists**.

Declaration of Independence

On June 11, 1776, Congress decided to move ahead on Lee's proposal. The members appointed a committee to draft a formal declaration of independence. In less than three weeks, the committee presented its final draft of the document. Congress formally accepted the Declaration of Independence on July 4, 1776. John Hancock was the first to sign his name to the new document. Every colony received a copy.

The document begins by stating that the colonists intend to cut ties with Britain and rule themselves. The second paragraph addresses the rights of the people to "life, liberty, and the pursuit of happiness." Next, the declaration lists many **grievances**. It explains why the colonies are separating from their British "parent." It goes on to warn that Great Britain should take the declaration seriously. The two countries were now enemies. It ends with a statement of hope that one day the two countries would be at peace.

Great Britain did not view the Declaration of Independence as an important document. The British government tried to dismiss it as something written by a few unhappy colonists.

GREAT BRITAIN RESPONDS

In response to the Declaration of Independence, Great Britain sent powerful warships up the Hudson River and into New York Harbor. British general William Howe and his brother Admiral Lord Richard Howe were in charge. The **fleet** included 30 battleships, 1,200 cannons, 30,000 soldiers, 10,000 sailors, and 300 supply ships.

| 1754–1763 | 1763–1773 | 1774–1775 | 1775 | 1776 | JUNE 11, |

JULY 4, 1

At 33 years old, Thomas Jefferson was the main author of the Declaration of Independence. He wrote the first draft in just one day. The term "United States of America" was first used in this document.

Jefferson was born in 1743. He became the nation's third president in 1801. He dedicated his life to the principle of freedom and died on July 4, 1826.

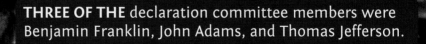

THREE OF THE declaration committee members were Benjamin Franklin, John Adams, and Thomas Jefferson.

Conflict Continues

The colonists spent the summer and fall of 1776 fighting for freedom. On August 27, General Washington's troops faced 15,000 British soldiers at the Battle of Long Island. They were badly beaten.

Washington's troops escaped across the East River during the night. Washington was the last to leave. He managed to avoid major battles by moving his men north out of New York City. In the fall, the Patriots saw further intense battles in other parts of New York.

In September, General Howe held peace talks with John Adams and Benjamin Franklin. The talks failed. Howe then demanded that the colonists **retract** the Declaration of Independence. The summer had been a low point for the Patriot cause, but they refused to back down.

ON THE NIGHT of December 25, 1776, George Washington led 2,400 troops across the Delaware River in an icy snowstorm. They landed at Trenton, New Jersey, at 3 AM. The Patriots surprised and outfought 1,400 Germans fighting for Great Britain. It was a great moment of victory for Washington.

| 1754–1763 | 1763–1773 | 1774–1775 | 1775 | 1776 | 1776 |

British Power

The British had several victories in the fall of 1776. In November, they attacked Fort Washington in Manhattan, capturing the arsenal there. Three days later, British general Charles Cornwallis drove Washington's forces out of Fort Lee in New Jersey. In December, British troops captured the naval base at Newport, Rhode Island.

BATTLE LOSSES

FORT WASHINGTON
British – 84 killed, 374 wounded
American – 59 killed, 96 wounded, 2,838 captured

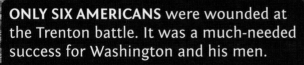

ONLY SIX AMERICANS were wounded at the Trenton battle. It was a much-needed success for Washington and his men.

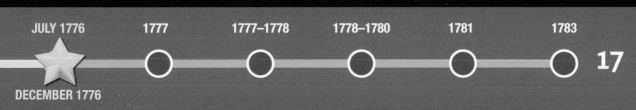

Victories and Losses

Slowly, the Patriots began to win more battles. On January 3, 1777, U.S. troops defeated the British at Princeton, New Jersey. They pushed the British back to New Brunswick.

That spring, the colonists won battles in New Jersey and Connecticut. They also suffered losses. In June 1777, British commander General John Burgoyne came south from Canada. He had 7,700 troops with him. In a surprise attack, they captured Fort Ticonderoga on Lake Champlain.

This was a big loss for Washington's troops. The British took all the fort's military supplies. In July 1777, however, Washington received important aid. A young Frenchman named Marquis de Lafayette volunteered to help the United States. Lafayette became General Washington's valuable assistant.

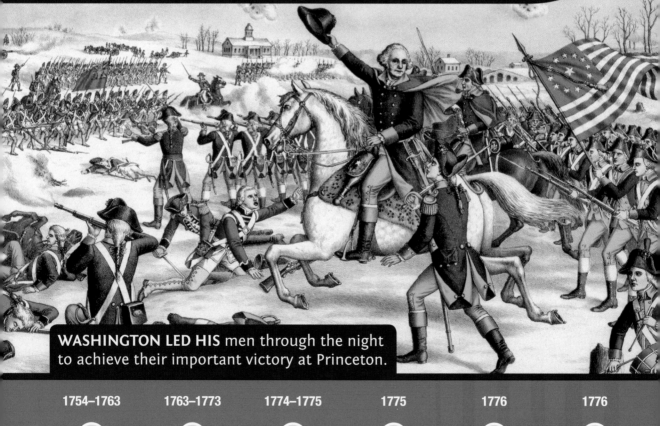

WASHINGTON LED HIS men through the night to achieve their important victory at Princeton.

| 1754–1763 | 1763–1773 | 1774–1775 | 1775 | 1776 | 1776 |

On October 7, 1777, U.S. troops experienced their first big success at the Battle of Saratoga in New York. Ten days later, British general Burgoyne **surrendered** to General Horatio Gates and General Benedict Arnold.

THE "STARS AND Stripes" became the first official flag of the United States on June 14, 1777. The flag design showed 13 white stars in a circle on a blue field. It had 13 alternating red and white stripes. The number of stars and stripes represented the 13 original U.S. colonies.

Valley Forge

In the fall of 1777, the British had taken control of the U.S. capital, Philadelphia. In response, Washington led 11,000 troops into battle at Germantown, Pennsylvania, on October 4. He hoped to overpower the British and bring the war to a sudden end. The British fought off the attack, and the U.S. troops withdrew.

With winter coming on, Washington set up camp in Valley Forge, Pennsylvania. It was a brutal place to spend a winter. Some soldiers fled after serving their time. Others **defected**. Those who remained built simple huts, their only shelter from the cold. Hundreds died of disease.

On February 6, 1778, U.S. delegates signed two treaties in Paris, France. One was the Treaty of Amity and Commerce. The other was the Treaty of Alliance. The treaties promised that the French would provide military supplies and join the fight against Great Britain. The French officially recognized the U.S. colonies as an independent country.

BARON VON STEUBEN

Baron von Steuben was a military leader from Prussia, a small country that later became part of Germany. Steuben arrived in Valley Forge on February 23, 1778. His job was to train the troops as professional military men. By May, the Continental Army was greatly improved.

Steuben began as a volunteer but rose in the ranks. He retired with honor from the U.S. military in March 1784.

| 1754–1763 | 1763–1773 | 1774–1775 | 1775 | 1776 | 1776 |

On March 16, 1778, British delegates traveled to Philadelphia. There, they offered to grant all U.S. demands but one. The country could not have its freedom. Congress rejected the offer.

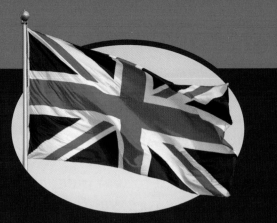

ON DECEMBER 19, 1777, about 11,000 U.S. troops marched to Valley Forge. Of these, 2,000 were barefoot. At camp, bitter cold, starvation, and lack of supplies made survival a triumph of human will. Some called Valley Forge a "camp of skeletons".

1776   1777   OCTOBER 4, 1777   1778–1780   1781   1783

MARCH 16, 1778

No Peace in Sight

During the American Revolution, even the colonists were divided. The sides were clear-cut. The Patriots were determined to win independence from Britain. Those loyal to King George wanted to remain British citizens. These Loyalists continued to recognize the king as their ruler. Many American Indians resented the American settlers. This gave them good reason to side with the British.

NOVEMBER 1778

In November 1778, Loyalists and American Indians killed more than 40 settlers at Cherry Valley, New York. In response, Patriot troops attacked Chickamauga Indian villages in Tennessee in April 1779.

AUGUST 1779

On August 29, 1779, the Patriots defeated the Loyalist and Indian troops at Elmira, New York. The Patriots destroyed nearly 40 Cayuga and Seneca Indian villages.

SEPTEMBER 1779

On September 27, 1779, Congress appointed John Adams to once again attempt peace talks with Britain.

OCTOBER 1779

In October 1779, General Washington set up his winter camp in Morristown, New Jersey. His troops endured another severe winter. **Morale** was low. Supplies were scarce. Many men deserted.

MAY 1780

The Patriots suffered their biggest material loss of the war on May 12, 1780. The British captured Charleston, South Carolina. In the **siege**, the Patriots lost their southern army, four ships, and guns and ammunition.

The Battle of Yorktown

By September 1781, British general Cornwallis had lost the Carolinas. He turned his attention to Virginia. In late September, he won Yorktown and Gloucester on opposite sides of the York River. The Patriots, led by General Washington, marched south. They met the British head on. With an army of almost 17,000 U.S. and French troops, Washington began taking over Yorktown.

By September 28, Washington's men surrounded Yorktown. The two sides fought for three weeks. General Cornwallis needed ammunition, food, and more men. French ships blocked the British from sending supplies or help. On October 19, 1781, Cornwallis led his men out of Yorktown and surrendered. It was the last major battle of the American Revolution. The colonists had won their independence.

WHEN IT CAME time to sign the official document of surrender at Yorktown, Cornwallis claimed to be ill. He sent someone else in his place.

| 1754–1763 | 1763–1773 | 1774–1775 | 1775 | 1776 | 1776 |

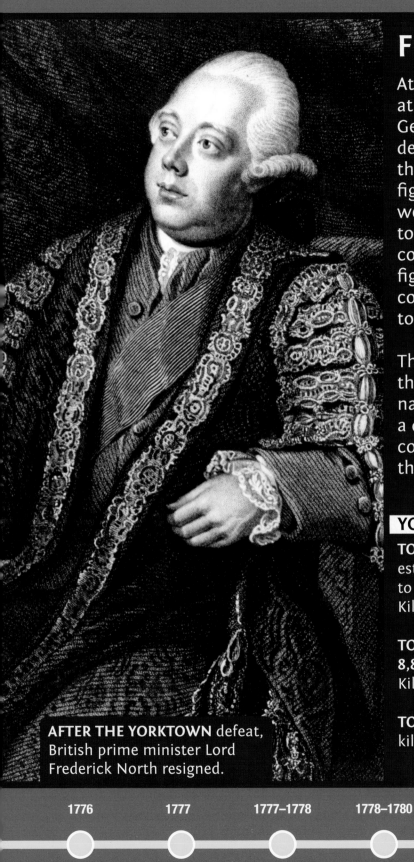

Final Loss

At the Battle of Yorktown, at least 6,000 British and German troops admitted defeat. The British realized then that continuing to fight was pointless. There were too many difficulties to overcome. The war was costly. The troops were fighting far from home. The colonists were determined to win their freedom.

The Yorktown siege was the final blow. The British nation gave up on waging a distant war. The U.S. colonies were not worth the cost.

YORKTOWN NUMBERS

TOTAL BRITISH TROOPS – estimates vary from 6,000 to 9,000
Killed or injured – 500

TOTAL AMERICAN TROOPS – 8,800
Killed or injured – 80

TOTAL FRENCH TROOPS – 7,800
killed or injured – 200

AFTER THE YORKTOWN defeat, British prime minister Lord Frederick North resigned.

The Treaty of Paris

The Revolutionary War battles had ended. Peace talks began in April 1782. Great Britain wanted an informal agreement. The United States insisted on a written agreement signed by both sides. The U.S. representatives argued fiercely for terms that would be good for their new nation.

In the 1783 Treaty of Paris, King George III agreed to recognize the 13 colonies as a new nation. The United States would govern itself, independent of Great Britain. The treaty also set new boundaries, which enlarged the size of the new nation. There were several other clauses that set the terms of the agreement. Even though both sides signed the agreement, some of the terms were ignored.

The treaty was signed on September 3, 1783. The signing officially marked the end of the American Revolutionary War. It was time for the Americans to determine what it meant to be a free and independent new nation.

The 1783 Treaty of Paris took two months to complete. It encouraged both Great Britain and the new United States to put aside their differences and return to being friends.

A GENERAL PEACE

NEW-YORK, March 25, 1783

LATE last Night, an EXPRESS from New-Jersey, brought the following Account.

THAT on Sunday last, the Twenty-Third Instant, a Vessel arrived at Philadelphia, in Thirty-five Days from Cadis, with Dispatches to the Continental Congress, informing them, that on Monday the Twentieth Day of January, the PRELIMINARIES to

A GENERAL PEACE,

Between Great-Britain, France, Spain, Holland, and the United States of America, were SIGNED at Paris, by all the Commissioners from those Powers; in consequence of which, Hostilities, by Sea and Land, were to cease in Europe, on Wednesday the Twentieth Day of February; and in America, on Thursday the Twentieth Day of March, in the present Year One Thousand Seven Hundred and Eighty-Three.

THIS very important Intelligence was last Night announced by the Firing of Cannon, and great Rejoicings at Elizabeth-Town.---Respecting the Particulars of this truly interesting Event no more are yet received, but they are hourly expected.

Published by James Rivington, Printer to the King's Most Excellent Majesty.

IN 1783, BENJAMIN Franklin, John Jay, and John Adams signed an official peace agreement with Great Britain in Paris, France.

Fill in the Blanks

Timelines are only a beginning. They provide an overview of the key events and important people that shaped history. Now, research in the library and on the internet to discover more about this period in the history of the United States.

A concept web can help you organize your ideas. Use the questions in the concept web to guide your research. When finished, use the completed web to help you write a report.

GEORGE WASHINGTON IS honored with memorials in cities across the United States.

Concept Web

People Involved
- Who was involved in this event?
- What were the professions of the people involved?
- How did they come to be involved in this event?

Historic Place
- Where did this event take place?
- What was unique about this place?
- What is in this location today?

Significant Events
- What happened?
- What did the key people do?

Research an Aspect of the American Revolution

Causes and Effects
- What caused the event?
- What were the immediate effects of the event that took place?
- What were the long–term effects of the event?

Problems and Solutions
- What were some of the problems that people experienced?
- How were they solved?

Brain Teaser

1. Which British general surrendered at Yorktown?

2. How many colonies fought for their independence from Great Britain in the American Revolution?

3. Which well-known Bostonian warned the Patriots that the British troops were coming?

4. Where did Washington and his troops spend the harsh winter of 1777–1778?

5. Who was commander-in-chief of the Continental Army?

6. Who came to Valley Forge to help train U.S. troops?

7. What signal told the Patriots whether the British troops were coming by land or by sea?

8. What was the last battle of the American Revolution?

9. What did Richard Henry Lee suggest that Congress should do?

10. Who was the king of Great Britain at the time of the American Revolution?

11. Who was the main author of the Declaration of Independence?

12. Who represented the United States at the signing of the 1783 Treaty of Paris?

Key Words

arsenal: a collection of weapons and ammunition; also, the place where these things are stored

colonies: areas that are under the control of another country

criticized: pointed out faults

declare: formally state or announce

defected: gave up a cause and left without permission

delegates: people sent to represent others at a meeting or conference

fleet: a large group of ships

grievances: complaints about unfair treatment

independence: freedom to decide things for oneself

loyalties: strong feelings of support for a particular country or cause

loyalists: early American colonists who wanted to remain loyal to Great Britain

parliament: the highest law-making body of the British government

Patriots: U.S. colonists who resisted being ruled by Great Britain

proclamation: an important public announcement

proposal: a suggestion or a formal plan

retract: take back

revolution: a forceful overthrow of one government in favor of another

Second Continental Congress: America's central governing body from 1775 to 1788

siege: a military operation in which a city is surrounded so it cannot get supplies

surrendered: gave up

textiles: fabric or cloth

treaty: a formal agreement between two or more nations

Index

Log on to www.av2books.com

AV[2] by Weigl brings you media enhanced books that support active learning. Go to www.av2books.com, and enter the special code found on page 2 of this book. You will gain access to enriched and enhanced content that supplements and complements this book. Content includes video, audio, weblinks, quizzes, a slide show, and activities.

AV[2] Online Navigation

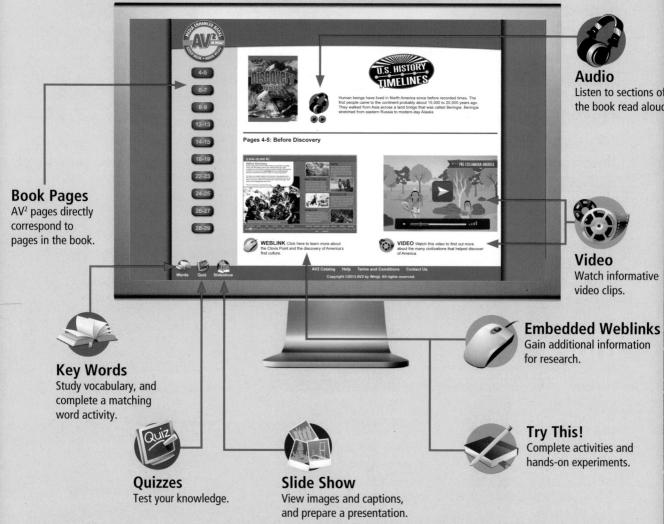

Audio
Listen to sections of the book read aloud.

Book Pages
AV[2] pages directly correspond to pages in the book.

Video
Watch informative video clips.

Key Words
Study vocabulary, and complete a matching word activity.

Embedded Weblinks
Gain additional information for research.

Try This!
Complete activities and hands-on experiments.

Quizzes
Test your knowledge.

Slide Show
View images and captions, and prepare a presentation.

AV[2] was built to bridge the gap between print and digital. We encourage you to tell us what you like and what you want to see in the future.

Sign up to be an AV[2] Ambassador at www.av2books.com/ambassador.

Due to the dynamic nature of the Internet, some of the URLs and activities provided as part of AV[2] by Weigl may have changed or ceased to exist. AV[2] by Weigl accepts no responsibility for any such changes. All media enhanced books are regularly monitored to update addresses and sites in a timely manner. Contact AV[2] by Weigl at 1-866-649-3445 or av2books@weigl.com with any questions, comments, or feedback.